Get the vet!

"Ben, Ben!
Bess is sick," yelled Pen.

Moo... moo

Moo

"Get Dad," said Pen,
"Bess is sick."

"Get Dad quick!" said Pen.

"Dad, Dad! Quick!
Bess is sick," yelled Ben.

"Quick, Dad, quick!"

Dad and Ben ran
to help Bess.

"Look Dad," said Pen,
"Bess is not well. Bess is sick.
Please help her Dad,
please help her."

"Ben, run and get Mum,"
said Dad.

"Pen, run and get the vet,"
said Dad.

Ben ran
and ran.

Pen ran and ran.

Dad sat with Bess.

"Mum!" yelled Ben.
"Quick! Bess is not well,
Bess is sick. Quick, quick!"

"Is the vet in?"

"Please tell the vet
Bess is not well," said Pen.

"Please tell the vet Bess is sick."

"But Bess is *not* sick,"
said Mum.

Quick Mum, quick!

"But Pen, Pen, Bess is *not*
sick!" yelled Mum.

"Bess is *very* sick,
 she is *very* sick," said Ben.

Pen ran back to Dad.

Ben ran back to Dad.

"Stop!" said Dad. "Stop!"

"Stop! *Sh… sh,*" said Dad.

"Help the vet," said Mum.
"Help the vet get his bags,"
said Mum.

"Is Bess still ill?" said Pen.

"No," said the vet.
"Bess is not ill."

"Bess is not sick. Look!"
said Mum. "Lick her Bess,"

"Moo... moo," went Bess.

It's gold!

"Help me Kim. Help me Tim.
Please help me down the cliff,"
said Miss Sim.

Tim and Kim like Miss Sim.

"Sit down, Miss Sim,"
said Kim.

"Sit down
and slip down," said Tim.

Miss Sim slid in the mud.
'Bang!' Down she went.

"Help me. Please help me!"
she yells.

Down went Spot.
Down went Spot
to help Miss Sim.

Spot likes Miss Sim.
He licks Miss Sim!
"Stop it Spot! Stop it!"
said Rob.

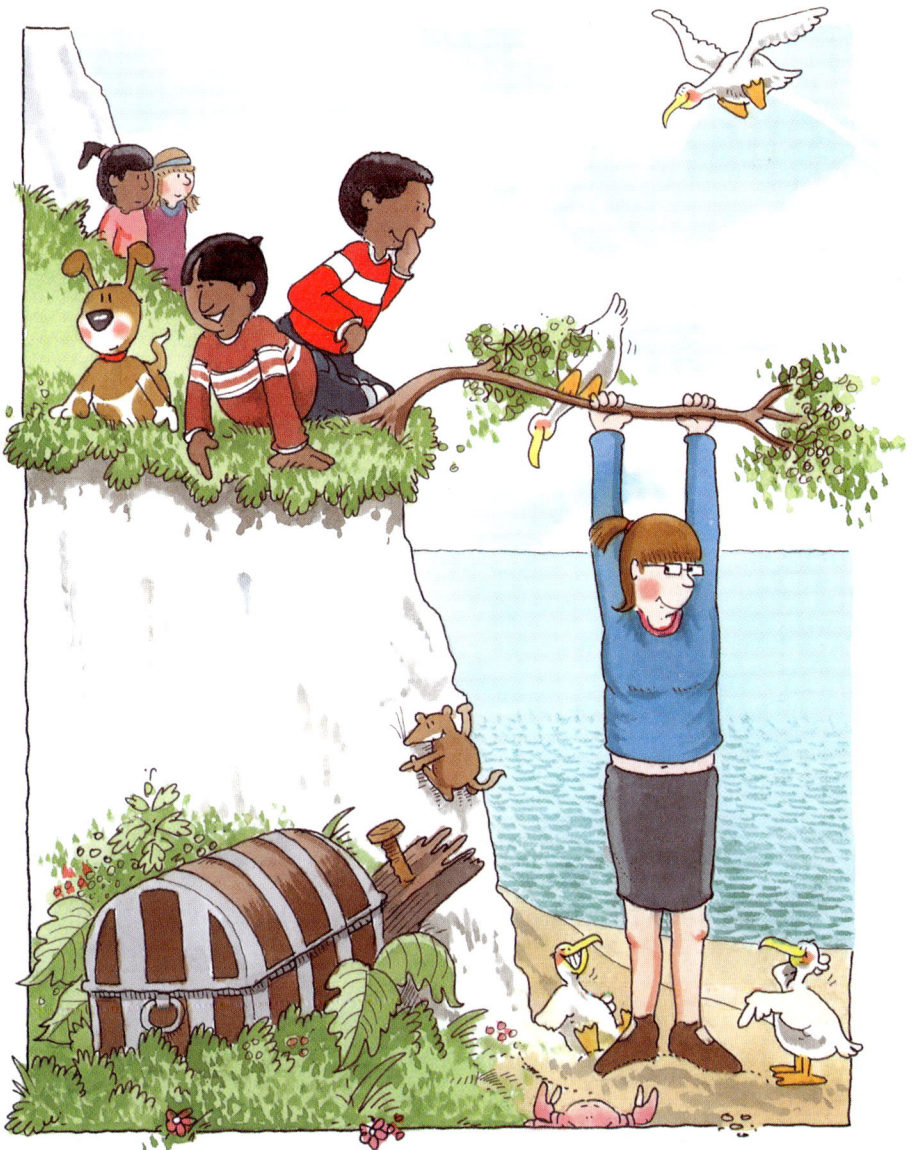

"Look Miss Sim. It's a trunk, a big, old trunk," said Ali.

"Can we get it?" said Trish.
"We can get it!" said Sue.

"Yes," said Miss Sim,
"but let Jack help."

"Lift it," said Jack.
"Lift the old trunk,
and I'll hold it with the rope."

"Is it gold, Jack?" said Trish.
"Is it gold in the old trunk?"

"Help get it up," said Jack.
"Let's get it to the top of
 the cliff."

They huff and they puff.

They puff and they huff.

28

Up… up… up.

Up the cliff went the big
old trunk.

Spot! Stop it! Stop it, Spot!

Bang...

bump...

bump...

bang...

Bash, crash! Down it went.

Bash...

crash...

splash!

Quick! Let's get the gold!